Know God, Know Peace

Devotional Artistic Photography
A.K. Ryan

ELM HILL

A Division of
HarperCollins Christian Publishing

www.elmhillbooks.com

Know God, Know Peace

Devotional Artistic Photography

Published in Nashville, Tennessee, by Elm Hill, an imprint of Thomas Nelson. Elm Hill and Thomas Nelson are registered trademarks of HarperCollins Christian Publishing, Inc.

Elm Hill titles may be purchased in bulk for educational, business, fund-raising, or sales promotional use. For information, please e-mail SpecialMarkets@ThomasNelson.com.

Publisher's Note: This novel is a work of fiction. Names, characters, places, and incidents are either products of the author's imagination or used fictitiously. All characters are fictional, and any similarity to people living or dead is purely coincidental.

Library of Congress Cataloging-in-Publication Data

Library of Congress Control Number: 2019912377

ISBN 978-1-400329182 (Paperback)
ISBN 978-1-400329199 (Hardbound)
ISBN 978-1-400329205 (eBook)

Know God,
Know Peace

May the God of Hope
fill you with all
Joy and Peace
as you trust in him,
so that you may overflow

with *hope* by the
power of the
Holy Spirit.

Romans 15:23 NIV

This is how I found God's peace.

- Author, A.K. Ryan

"The peace we seek in the world cannot appear until its flame is first lit in our hearts."

"It is a divine force that whispers gently but insistently, coaxing us ever deeper into the dark recesses of our soul, shedding its healing light and liberating us from our fears."

- Mony Agraso
Walking for Peace

SEEK THE

Kingdome of God

ABOVE ALL ELSE

Matthew 6:33, NLT

Grace and Peace
be yours in abundance through the knowledge of
God and of Jesus our Lord.

2 Peter 1:2 NIV

Keep your mind set on God's will.

"If our minds are stayed upon God,
His peace will rule the affairs
entertained by our minds.
If, on the other hand, we allow our minds
to dwell on the cares of this world,
God's peace will be far from our thoughts."

- Woodrow Kroll

Seek his will in all you do and he will show you which path to take.

Proverbs 3:6

"Knowing we will be with Christ forever
far outweighs our burdens today!
Keep our eyes on eternity!"

- Billy Graham

"*Seek true Peace*
not in earth, but in heaven;
not in men, nor in any other creature,
but in God alone."

- Thomas Kempis

Set your minds on things above

not on earthly things.

Colossians 3:2

"In thus following the Spirit they invariably shall *set their minds on the things of the Spirit.* And the result shall be *life and peace."*

- Watchman Nee

For those who live according to the flesh set their minds on the things of the flesh, *but those who live according to the Spirit,* set their minds on the things of the Spirit.

For to set the mind on the flesh is death, *but to set the mind on the Spirit is life and peace.*

Romans 8:5-6 ESV

"The world can create
Trouble in Peace

but God can create
Peace in trouble."

- Thomas Watson

"*Because of the favor of God*
we can have peace in the midst of chaos."

- Crystal McDowell

Peace is not the
absence of trouble,
but the presence of
Christ.

- Sheila Walsh

"A great many people are trying to make peace,
but that has already been done.
God has not left it for us to do;
all we have to do is to enter into it."

- Dwight L. Moody

Realize God's peace
by first proclaiming
Jesus as your Lord and Savior.

- Author A.K. Ryan

Count your blessings
instead of your crosses;
your gains instead
of your losses.
Your joys instead
of your woes;
your friends instead
of your foes.
Your smiles instead
of your tears;
your courage instead
of your fears.
Your full years
instead of your lean;
your kind instead
of your mean.
Your health instead
of your wealth;

Count on God instead of yourself

-Irish blessing

I have told you these things so you may have Peace.

In this world you will have trouble.
But take heart! I have overcome the world.

John 14:27 ESV

" *If you're missing joy and peace,*
you're not trusting God. "

- Joyce Meyer

TRUST
in the Lord
with all your
HEART

trust
Jesus

"If God, be our God, He will give us peace in trouble.
When there is a storm without, He will make peace within."

- Thomas Watson

"God sweetens outward pain with inward peace."

- Thomas Watson

The Lord
will guide you along
the path he intends for you

"Direct me in the path of your commands,
for there I find delight."

Psalm 119:35 NIV

Dear Lord,
In your strong hands,
I place my life.
Choosing to depend on you
to light and guide my path.

I am The
Light
of The
World

John 8:12

"Darkness cannot drive out darkness:
only light can do that.
Hate cannot drive out hate:
only love can do that."

- Martin Luther King Jr.

Love is patient and kind;
love does not envy or boast;
it is not arrogant or rude.
It does not insist on its own way;
it is not irritable or resentful;
it does not rejoice in wrongdoing,
but rejoices with the truth.
Love bears all things, believes all things,
hopes all things, endures all things.
love never ends.

1 Corinthians 13:4-8 ESV

don't worry about tomorrow
for tomorrow will
bring its own worries,
today's trouble is
enough for today.

Matthew 6:34

"Time spent worrying drains your energy.
It makes you weaker. You are created to live a peace-filled life."

- Joel Osteen

Don't worry about anything;
instead
Pray about everything,

tell God what you need,
and thank him for all he has done.

Philippians 4:6

"*You don't have to worry or be stressed out.*
Stay in peace.
God is directing your steps.
He controls the universe."

- Joel Osteen

"*Because of the empty tomb, we have peace.*
Because of His resurrection, we can have peace
during even the most troubling of times,
because we know He is in control of all
that happens in the world."

- Paul Chappell

And we know that in all things
God works for the good
of those who love him,
who have been called

according to his purpose

Romans 8:28
NIV

With God All Things Are Possible.

Matthew 19:26

I WILL
FEAR NO EVIL,
FOR YOU ARE
With Me

PSALM 23:4 NIV

Have I not commanded you? Be strong and courageous.

Do not be afraid; do not be discouraged,
for the Lord your God will be with you
wherever you go.

Joshua 1:9 NIV

So do not fear, for I am with you; do not be dismayed, for I am your God.

I will strengthen you and help you;
I will uphold you with my rightous right hand.

Isaiah 41:10 NIV

With a steadfast faith there is comfort in
knowing that God is near.
No longer I but Christ in me,
I no longer fear uncertainty for I
am safe in the shadow of the Lord's love.

- Author A.K. Ryan

When I am afraid,
I put my trust in you,
for you are near.

My son, do not let wisdom and understanding out of your sight,
preserve sound judgment and discretion;
they will be life for you,
an ornament to grace your neck.

Then you will go on your way in safety,
and your foot will not stumble.
When you lie down, you will not be afraid;
when you lie down, your sleep will be sweet.

Have no fear of sudden disaster or of the
ruin that overtakes the wicked,
for the Lord will be at your side
and will keep your foot from being snared.

Proverbs 3:21-26 NIV

"I do not want the peace which passeth understanding, I want the understanding which bringeth peace."

- Helen Keller

"Peace cannot be kept by force; it can only be achieved by understanding."

- Albert Einstein

God grant me

Serenity
to accept the things I cannot change,

Courage
to change the things I can,

Wisdom
to know the difference.

Each one of us has been given the gift of God's grace.

"For by grace you have been saved through faith. And this is not your own doing; it is the gift of God."

Ephesians 2:8 ESV

My grace is
all you need

My power works
best in weakness.

2 CORINTHIANS 12:9

*"Prayer girds human weakness
with divine strength,*
turns human folly into heavenly wisdom,
and gives to troubled mortals the
peace of God."

- Charles Spurgeon

Pray
in the power of the
Holy Spirit

Jude 1:20

"Only God can give us a selfless
love for others
as the *Holy Spirit*
changes us from within.

This is one reason we must receive *Christ*,
for apart from His Spirit we can never
be freed from the chains of selfishness,
jealousy and indifference."

- Billy Graham

Grow flowers of gratitude in the soil of prayer

Speak to God in prayer.
God speaks to you through his Word.

- Author, A.K. Ryan

PRAYER *everything* CHANGES

Never doubt the power of prayer.

Prayer is exchanging
our worries
for his wisdom,

our pain for his peace,

our confusion
for his confidence.

Prayer is the road to heaven, but faith opens the door.

"*Choosing an attitude of faith* will release peace out of your spirit and into your soul."

- Joyce Meyer

prayer is bringing your worries & wishes to God *faith* is leaving them there.

Your heart is the sun.

Abundant joy, its stars.

Faith is the moon,

shining in your
darkness.

Life without
faith is like
being in a boat
without oars.

FAITH CAN MOVE MOUNTAINS,
BUT DON'T BE SURPRISED IF
GOD HANDS YOU A SHOVEL.

Having faith in God means trusting
in God's promises, and knowing
without any doubt
that during your trials in life,
He will make it for good.

- Author, A.K. Ryan

God's promises
are like stars,
the darker
the night the
brighter they shine.

"We are not at peace with others
because we are not at peace with ourselves,
and we are not at peace with ourselves
because we are not at peace with God."

- Thomas Merton

"No one can have the peace of God
until they are at peace with God."

- Jack Wellman

No God, No Peace
Know God, Know Peace

"Happiness without peace is temporal; Peace along with happiness is eternal."

- James H. Aughey

"*God cannot give us happiness and peace*
apart from Himself, because it is not there.
There is no such thing."

- C.S. Lewis

Let my teaching fall like rain

and my words descend like dew, like showers on new grass,
like abundant rain on tender plants.

I will proclaim the name of the Lord.

Deuteronomy 32:2-3 NIV

"Rejoice in the Lord always. I will say it again: Rejoice!"

Let your gentleness be evident to all. The Lord is near.
Do not be anxious about anything,
but in every situation, by prayer and petition,
with thanksgiving, present your requests to God.
And the peace of God, which transcends all understanding,
will guard your hearts and your minds in Jesus Christ.

- Philppians 4:3-7

Glory to God in the highest heaven,
and on earth peace to those
whom his favor rests.

- Luke 2:14

May the *peace* of God
be with you
always

Peace I leave with you;
my peace I give to you.
Not as the world gives do I give to you.
Let not your hearts be troubled,
neither let them be afraid.

John 14:27 ESV

Now may the Lord of peace himself
give you peace at all times
and in every way.

2 Thessalonians 3:16 NIV

Finally, brothers and sisters,
whatever is true,
whatever is noble,
whatever is right,
whatever is pure,
whatever is lovely,
whatever is admirable--
if anything is excellent
or praiseworthy--
think about such things.
Whatever you have learned
or received or heard from me,
or seen in me--
put it into practice.
And the God of Peace will be with you.

Philippians 4:8-9 NIV

Peace be with you.

Dear Lord,

Please help me keep my thoughts on eternity and to not focus on the troubles of this world. That I may seek the Kingdome of Heaven above all else. Show me which path to take that will please you. With a world full of choices and difficult decisions I will depend on you to guide me; I will count on you instead of myself. I accept that peace is not the absence of trouble, but the presence of Christ, and I will enter into your peace because I know you are a God of love. You are my Lord and Savior and with you all things are possible.

Help me to not fear uncertainty and to have courage for I know you are always near. I trust in your promises; I believe that you are the light in my darkness. I recognize that my life without faith would be missing joy and peace and purpose. Thank you for your grace, for my abundant blessings, and your unconditional love.

Help me find the peace only you can give. Amen

CPSIA information can be obtained
at www.ICGtesting.com
Printed in the USA
LVHW072036131119
637306LV00007B/10/P